Emotional Intelligence in School

Juan Moisés de la Serna

www.juanmoisesdelaserna.es/en

Translated by: Susana Hyder

Preface

When we talk about emotional intelligence, we are actually referring to the development of the person. This topic has been on the rise for a few decades and it has proven to be useful not only on a personal level but also in the workplace.

Research on the benefits of a proper development of Emotional Intelligence is on the increase, advising on the training of it as early as possible.

Therefore, school is the most suitable environment for young children and even adolescents to get to know and to develop Emotional Intelligence.

Index

Dedicated to my parents

Acknowledgements

I would like to take this opportunity to thank all the people who collaborated with their contributions towards the completion of this book. Particularly the Government of Canarias, and Dr. Noelia Carbonell Bernal.

Legal Notice

This book may not be reproduced in its entirety or in part, uploaded to any information storage and retrieval system, or transmitted in any form by any means, whether electronic or mechanical, including photocopying, by recording or any other means without prior and written permission from the author and copyright owner. Infringement of the aforementioned rights may constitute a criminal offense under intellectual legislation. (Art. 270 ff of the Penal Code). Refer to C.E.D.R.O. (Centro Español de Derechos Reprográficos) if you need to photocopy or scan any portion of this work. You may contact C.E.D.R.O. online at www.conlicencia.com or by phone at 91 702 19 70 / 93 272 04 47.

© Juan Moisés de la Serna, 2018
Translated by: Susana Hyder

Chapter 1. Emotional Intelligence

It can be said we live in an emotional world just as it can be said we live in a social world. Therefore, those who are more skilled at their emotional development tend to be the most successful. For example, a merchant of any product or service is mainly concerned with selling emotions so the other person will buy or acquire that which he is selling.

The media, television, radio or any other advertising means target the emotions and with that they aim to sell their products or services. But not everyone has the same level of emotional ability. There are some people that for some reason do not sufficiently achieve this ability. Hence, a new area of research and work in psychology was initiated a few years ago by Daniel Goleman namcd Emotional Intelligence together with a book written with the same title.

Intelligence has been traditionally defined as the ability to satisfactorily answer a series of standardized questionnaire designed for a specific "target class"determined by genetics.

This means the questionnaire or test has been validated by small trials before being administered to the general population and it is valid internally and externally, in other words, measures what needs to be measured in addition to being specially designed for a determined collective and age range.

Even though the use of intelligence questionnaires emerged in the XIX century there has been much criticism as they have been considered "unfair" because they are designed to evaluate entire populations using the same standards.

In the beginning of the last century there was much controversy about the research conducted by the army to analyze the relationship between intelligence and race. The   results of the American population were analyzed in relation   to whether the participant was white or black, and between Native Americans and immigrants.   The conclusion was that   whites of Anglo-Saxon origin had better results than other racial groups and of immigrants whose mother tongue was not English. This prompted a modification   of   education   policies   geared   towards "compensating" for such differences.

Subsequent studies debunked these results due to flaws in the tests used which did not take into account the correct jargon of the target group of people being tested thus making it necessary to adapt the test according to who it was given to.

In spite of this, the intelligence quotient continues to be a validated measure of problem solving abilities by means of tests designed and prepared by psychologists who follow strict regulation standards established by psychometrics (science of measuring) so that the results are valid and reliable for the population to which they are given.

Thanks to this the academic success and professional future of students can be predicted way before they are even aware of their abilities and potentials. They are likewise used in the field of personnel selection for finding the ideal candidate for a position who would not necessarily have to be the one with the most qualifications or experience.

Through the years the field of psychometrics has been perfected and improved to the point where its reliability is quite high. This is the reason why some businesses decide their "future" based on the results of the evaluations performed by Human Resources.

Intelligence evaluation is a controversial topic not only because of its definition but also because of what it entails. In regards to its definition, there are some who would bundle intelligence as a single construct, in other words, either you are intelligent or you are not. If you are, you can belong to the "bunch" or be below the mean or above. If you belong to the latter you may be more intelligent than the rest, a prodigy or a genius to varying degrees.

This would be the case if we continued to follow the classic model of intelligence which is now obsolete.

However, the concept of intelligence has been

questioned in the last few decades due to the understanding that it is not a standard value but rather that there are many different types of intelligences: spatial intelligence, verbal intelligence, mathematic intelligence, musical intelligence, etc.

A person who has a highly developed ability for music may be a great "Chopin" or "Mozart" of our days but he may not be able to shine when it comes to solving for example, integrals, derivatives or trigonometry.

Something else that is different is the "genius", able to stand out in many of these aspects of intelligence; even though to date there is no scientific consensus to clearly establish this distinction.

Another aspect is the social implications of the highly gifted, feared by some and desired by others. Some countries have spent years investing much effort in populating screening, in other words, intelligence questionnaires administered to all the schools to detect those "potential geniuses".

Likewise, the universities, especially those who are high ranking in the world are attentive to those students who excel in high school to offer them all kinds of opportunities to study in their facilities knowing that most of them will end up being professors or researchers in their staff in the future.

In spite of the aforementioned, in the majority of the cases, the main challenge for parents and teachers is that the child is able to take advantage of the education phase beyond passing their grades.

When the main activity of children and adolescents is just attending classes, the academic results seem to be the best indicator of their progress.

Any parent would worry when seeing low academic performance. They would look for solutions whether this is finding a private tutor or limiting the child's play time.

In the same manner, when a child fails a grade, having to repeat it, the parents view this as a personal failure since they know that in the long rung this will affect the future of their child.

Instead of this situation becoming a "second opportunity" it turns into a problem furor the child as he sees himself labeled as "held back"forced to be in school with children younger than they are while he sees his former classmates progressing in their studies.

There are many factors that could make the child fix his attitude and performance to rectify that which causes him to fail academically. Can good academic performance be predicted?

This is the subject of research by the Faculty of Psychology, Padjadjaran University (Indonesia) together with the Busoga University (Uganda) whose results were published in The Open Psychology Journal.

The study tested 101 students. All of them filled out two standardized questionnaires; the Academic Self-Efficacy Questionnaire and the Regulated Learning Questionnaire to evaluate self-efficacy and self-regulation respectively.

Self-efficacy is defined as one's belief in one's own abilities; while self-regulation helps a person plan and achieve his goals; furthermore they gathered the academic grades of the last semester completed. The results indicate positive significant differences in the academic grades in relation to self-efficacy and self-regulation, that is, the more self-efficacy, the better the grades. Conversely, the less self-regulation meant poor academic results. There exists a positive correlation between self-efficacy and self-regulation.

The results do not provide information as to the relation between the two variables and academic performance.

It could be inferred that the students that have higher levels of self esteem and self regulation would have better academic performance but the study does not reveal that detail.

In spite of the accuracy of the results it bears considering that there are other variables that were not considered that could affect academic performance.

However, even with the aforementioned limitations the data offers an important breakthrough regarding intervention in academic failure.

Now, the results can be improved by intervening not only during the hours dedicated to study but also by developing self-efficiency and self-regulation abilities in the students.

In the first instance, by teaching the child about their true potential and the importance of behaving according to their way of thinking in order to build a better future.

In the second instance, by re-educating their behavioral habits, teaching them how to plan, prioritize and make their plans come to fruition.

It would be expected that with either one of these two simple interventions that the students' grades would improve. This aspect is yet to be proven in further research.

Chapter 2. Emotional Intelligence and Academic Performance

As has already been mentioned, the importance of intelligence evaluation as an intellectual coefficient factor, which can predict from infancy the academic development and later on in the workplace, allows for "selecting" between those who would be more "productive" in society and those who may not be.

This idea has been rejected by a large majority of the community who see this as a "sentence" to those less gifted, those who are labeled as "disabled", only because they do not perform the same as their peers.

In a society where success is measured by what a person is able to achieve sometimes, persons with an intellectual disability seem to not "fit in" when in reality these are the people who contribute to human diversity just the same a blondes or dark skinned people do, or tall, or short, and so on.

It would be the same as rejecting persons because they are dark skinned, or short, or stocky, in other words, just because they do not meet the "idealized" expectations of what a productive person should be like.

This is an issue that still needs to be overcome since nowadays there is still discrimination when it comes to hiring a person who is intellectually disabled for a job that they are very well qualified to perform.

Furthermore, in recent years there has been a shift in focus adopting other approaches to intelligence not only centered on an intelligence quotient. Thus the concept of Emotional Intelligence, which makes reference to our ability to relate to others, has been given special attention. Thanks to the emotional world that surrounds us, this intelligence seems to be determined initially by early experiences and greatly depends on the mother-to-child relation and family education style.

With time, experience, contact with others, and trial and error it will cause us to respond in one way or another to our own emotions and those of others.

Contrary to common belief, people who were not able to show their emotions in an appropriate way according to the situation can be trained to develop and improve the ability to be able to face any situation and know how to behave accordingly.

This ability has direct repercussions in social relations that are based on empathy, fellowship and intimacy.

Every time we encounter and have a conversation with a person we awaken various different emotions and the way we manage those emotions could have a direct effect on a business transaction or the beginning of a relationship.

Even though the majority of these random encounters will not have much impact on our lives, an adequate development of Emotional Intelligence will help in making these a pleasant experience and not stressful or challenging situations.

The type of Emotional Intelligence that refers to the ability of a person to listen to their bodies, in other words, listen to their emotions and adequately relate to their environment also makes reference to the ability to observe, understand and interpret emotions in others and be able to respond adequately to others as well.

Regarding the "origin" of intelligence and after many arguments between those who defended environmental reasons as opposed to those who attributed it to genetics, it is now believed that 80% of intelligence is genetics and that the development and potentiality of the remaining 20% is a product of effort and dedication. A joint study by the University of Amsterdam, the Vrije Universiteit Amsterdam and Tilburg University (Netherlands) whose results have been published in the scientific journal Psychological Science ran a bibliographical analysis of 23 previous studies on this subject. The results of this study contradict current dominant theories about intelligence, indicating that genetics have a greater value due to the homogeneity effect of the culture where one lives which affects predetermined developments that remain through time in a determined place.

In other words, genetics play a larger role than that which is attributed to it because people grow up in an environment that does not change with time.

Going back to Emotional Intelligence and based on the aforementioned, it can be said that a person is born with either greater or lesser ability even though he or she could learn and improve through social experience regardless of the level at the start. People with great Emotional Intelligence are able to understand others with barely a word, which is also labeled as having greater empathy. On the other hand, there are those with very little, if any, Emotional Intelligence far removed from being able to even understand their own emotions or to properly interpret the emotions of others.

The most well known practical application in the field of Emotional Intelligence is coaching. Geared towards helping people find their own values and motivations to reach their goals, it is now being applied to many areas in the work field, in business, sports or even health.

"Coaching promotes change, in order to improve and maintain health a people need to change their attitude and behavior. Health affects us all directly or indirectly (family illness) at one time or another in our lives.

According the definition by the WHO (World Health Organization):

'Health is a state of complete physical, mental and social well-being and not merely the absence of disease or infirmity'.

If we take into consideration this wide concept maybe we will find an area in our lives where we see room for improvement. It is good to reflect on that even though we may think we are healthy. Since coaching uses questions I take advantage of this to pose questions to the reader that have to do with psycho-social areas: Do I have friends? Do I have time to associate with them? Do I dedicate time each week for relaxation and to take care of myself? Improving in these areas is to invest in our health in addition to following a specific treatment in the case of illness."

Dr. Jaci Molins Roca Director of Post-Graduate Training in Personal Coaching and Organization at the Universitat Rovira i Vigili.

Emotional Intelligence requires basic and superior cognitive processes through which one gathers and interprets the external and internal world as well as modulates the expression of the emotions that are communicated. Hence the need to itemize each one to know in what measure they affect and how they begin to improve with practice and development of Emotional Intelligence.

In order to achieve normal development of Emotional Intelligence it is imperative that it is supported by the cognitive processes which initially allow the process of sensory information, external as well as internal, to perceive it and analyze it in order to produce an adequate response. This process becomes complicated when other processes are introduced, such as memory, attention, emotion or learning. There are many theoretical models that explain the workings of processing:

-Automatic vs. Controlled, which explains whether information analysis is intentional or not. The automatic processes being those related to the survival of an individual and that require a quick response such as jerking your hand back from a hot surface before even being "conscious" of it.

Emotional processing pathways are and example of automatic processing where there is no realization until after the stimulus is roughly analyzed and it is determined whether they are dangerous or not. Likewise, in reflex responses the frontal areas, or seat of the "central executive, responsible for planning and decision making are not involved.

- Serial vs. Parallel, which would indicate if only one dimension of the information is being processed or various at the same time. Obviously serial processing requires greater attentional resources. Emotional processing is also an example of parallel processing of sensory information which is distributed in parallel through this pathway and the conscious pathway which is slower and more detailed in its analysis.

- Below/Above vs. Above/Below, according to the processing being guided by sensory information (guided by data) or if it is derived from previous expectations and interpretations (conceptually guided).

An example of processing guided by below/above data is reading, where characters that make up a word are identified regardless of whether they appear on paper, a tablet, or with different font types.

The "translation" of those characters on paper, that make up letters, which in turn form words, which become phrases, messages and finally transmit ideas, is an example of above/below processing, since it requires a superior processing to give meaning to such stimuli.

-Global vs. Local indicates the type of processing more or less focused in parts or the whole.

Even though these types of processes have been presented in a dichotomous fashion they usually work simultaneously thus enriching the handling of information

Sensation is considered a necessary, previous step to

many cognitive processes through sensory receptors distribute throughout the body which can be divided as follows:

Exteroceptors; which correspond to the senses.

Propioceptors; that provide information about musculature and balance.

Interoceptors; that extend over glands and internal organs.

Cutaneous receptors; that allow the sensations of cold, heat, pressure, contact and pain.

Sensation is the first and fundamental step for any cognitive process without which none of the other processes would develop including emotional intelligence.

According to their functions they can be categorized as follows:

Photoreceptors, located in the eyes.

Mechanoreceptors, located in the ears and skin.

Thermoreceptors, found in the skin.

Chemoreceptors, found in the nose and tongue.

Information is gathered by neurons in the peripheral nervous system which is then sent to the central nervous system through the spinal cord and then if it gets through the attentional filter is integrated, processed and turned into conscious information.

Lack of senses can be observed in some disabilities

where sensorial information can be partially or completely lost which is often compensated by the overdevelopment of other senses.

Even though these are automatic processes and are not arbitrated by the level of intelligence development, it has been confirmed that highly gifted people are more sensitive than others. This condition has been named hyperesthesia which can be explained as improved connections in the neural network as well as the process of myelination which allows a much more rapid and effective transmission of information making the body more sensitive to environmental or internal changes

Without attention there are not very many cognitive processes or even emotional intelligence since both have to do with a previous process for which it is necessary to have a certain amount of "will" or at least intention, being in the "here and now", without which learning could not happen and as a result emotional intelligence could not be developed.

Furthermore it is an inverse relation, in the sense that the development of emotional intelligence will also guide the attention towards essential aspects of communication for example, the body language in a conversation that aid in interpreting emotions so adjustments can be made in communication.

Attention enables us to select and focus on relevant

information, separating it from that which is irrelevant concentrating resources only on the processing of significant events. This process could be divided in our ability to understand, concentrate and keep alert.

Regarding attention pathways and following the ideas of Posner we need to distinguish between:

-Attention as a general state of alert of the body which involves the locus coeruleus and also the frontal and parietal areas of the right hemisphere.

-The posterior attentional system, where attention and consciousness of sensory information is directed which involves the parietal and posterior lobes and the thalamus together with the superior mesencephalic colliculi.

- The anterior attentional system dealing with complex cognitive tasks, utilizing both sensory information and memory. This process is handled by the medial frontal areas of the cortex, the anterior cingulate area, the supplementary motor area and the basal ganglia.

In the highly gifted, maturation and the majority of the myelination of the frontal lobes occurs during early childhood. This enhances the system of activation and inhibition of selective attention which enables the child to have better attention and concentration in the assigned tasks and, when it comes to selecting stimulus, a better inhibition of irrelevant stimuli. When optimized, this process enables the body's saving of resources thus improving the ability to process information in this way avoiding overstimulation and system collapse as is the case with patients of schizophrenia.

It bears highlighting the perceived contradiction that some school aged children with high levels of intelligence could suffer from attention deficit in class. But this is not due to a lack of aptitude or reduced maturation of the neural system but rather a lack of motivation that leads to boredom when they have to attend classes that they are already familiar with or having understood what the teacher explained to begin with and then have to listen to the teacher repeat the lesson over and over again so the rest of the class can understand.

A scarce development of emotional intelligence would cause a person to get "lost" in unnecessary details or to not know how to "read signals" of the person with whom they are having a conversation and thus losing part of the emotional content of the conversation. Training the emotional intelligence includes developing a mindfulness of signals, expressions, and gestures as well as tone of voice through which the emotions of others can be interpreted in order to adjust our behavior accordingly.

To perceive is a complex process that is influenced by sensation, memory, and also prior expectations and is on this last point that emotional intelligence comes into play.

Our beliefs and expectations are modulated by our emotional intelligence so that the more developed it is the more flexibility and tolerance we would have towards the feelings and behaviors of others.

This is due to the characteristic of emotional intelligence, put oneself in the place the other and to assume or at least respect his point of view, something that no doubt would indicate the perception of each one. Perception, takes information from the senses (sight, hearing, smell, taste and touch) and elaborates on it in order to make representations with meaning which helps to understand reality and respond to it. It must be taken into account, that perception does not return a copy of reality, but that is a subjective representation of the same. For this purpose, different principles are used such as figure-ground relationship, grouping and constancy. There are various neural specialized areas based on the information perceived. Therefore, visual information is analyzed in the visual cortex, located in the occipital lobe; auditory information in the auditory cortex, which together with the olfactory information, in the olfactory bulb, is analyzed in the temporal lobe. In other pathways, information related to taste and touch is analyzed in the somatosensory cortex in the parietal lobe.

Perception is a fundamental component in the development of a person in the world in order to understand the environment which surrounds them and even the role one plays in it, as well as making our world "predictable" by understanding the rules it abides by. This factor has been evidenced by errors in perception, such as selective attention (only paying attention to the stimuli that are interesting to the person), stereotypes (excessive simplification of a category), halo effect (assessing a biased value of a person or a situation based on their characteristics), or projections (outwardly attributing to others what is felt or thought on the inside), among others.

An underdeveloped emotional intelligence would cause a person to not understand and assume that others have their own points of view, feelings and emotions and thus try to impose their own opinions on others. The development of emotional intelligence includes the training of the ability to "put yourself in someone else's shoes"and in this way be able to understand how he feels, what are his concerns or desires, all of which modulates our own behavior in order to adjust it depending on the person we are talking to.

Emotional intelligence cannot be developed without memory since this is a process that is learned with practice and that helps a person to know how to act in a changing social environment. In order to this it is necessary to be able to "grab ahold" of our memories to know how to act in each instance.

Keep in mind that one of the characteristics of emotional intelligence is that of adjusting the expression of emotions according to the context and this cannot be done without applying what has been learned.

Memory is the process of encoding, storage and retrieval of information. This process in influenced significantly by attention and emotion. The former, deals with selecting, storing and retrieving information and the latter, emotion, is related to the emotion associated with said memory.

It is very difficult to retrieve something that has not been given attention to as is the case with information that has been processed as irrelevant and as such has not created an imprint, thus remaining in the short term memory soon to be substituted by new information in a matter of minutes or seconds, following the model of Atkinson and Shiffrin who separates the memory process into: sensory memory, short term memory and long term memory.

The regions implicated in memory are many, such as the hippocampus, the thalamus, the amygdala of the temporal lobe, the mammillary bodies and even the cerebellum.

A greater neural density and greater interneuronal connections in the frontal areas allow for faster processing which increases the efficiency of the working memory which has to do with abstract thinking and creativity.

Likewise, it has been established that there is a close, positive relation between working memory and level of intelligence. There are people who are able to remember any event as if they were still there, this is called hypermnesia. Based on this, there have been many techniques developed to help these people to forget irrelevant events or information by weakening memory imprints until they disappear.

A person with little development of emotional intelligence would act the same way in a funeral as in a party due to their inability to remember how they are supposed to behave emotionally in each occasion. Role-play training, where a person is exposed to various fictitious situations, is crucial for emotional intelligence. In these sessions the person learns how they are expected to act in each circumstance and "memorizes" their experience so it can be used at a later time when the occasion arises.

.Motivation is the "motor" that justifies initiating or maintaining an activity promoting in the academic environment discovery and curiosity for learning more avoiding environments that do not provide enrichment and preferring those that pose a certain level of challenge.

As a counterpoint, motivation could turn into frustration if the environment in which is developed is not enriching enough, or if the person is not able to measure their potential with the adequate development of self regulation which would enable him to set realistic goals and in doing so guiding oneself through the proper steps in order to reach them, all this can be attributed to the motivation the person feels to improve,

Motivation is intricately related to emotional intelligence, since it is in an emotional world that a person becomes who they are, and the development of emotional intelligence is the guiding force behind this drive.

To know one's own emotions, what we like or dislike, be able to prioritize them and give them an outlet through actions can only be achieved because of the combination of emotional intelligence and motivation.

There have been other concepts based on this one such as: need (internal deficit), impulse (motivated need intensity), satiety (decrease in motivation); that is to say, conduct is motivated, action is initiated by impulse brought on by a need and once that need is satisfied it brings on satiety and fulfills such need.

Regarding physiological needs the hypothalamus takes care of regulating water and food intake as well as sleep regulation, aggressiveness, and sexual conduct. It is due to the afferent and efferent connections that these needs are carried out motivating action until they are satisfied.

Each "satisfactory" action, whether it is eating, drinking, sleeping, or having sex will produce a subjective sensation of reward when they are carried out which becomes a reinforcement of that behavior and a "motivator" of repetition thus initiating a motivation-reward cycle which is neurologically sustained. In 1954 Olds and Milner discovered that the ventral tegmental area (VTA) which is connected to the nucleus accumbens, the terminal stria, the amygdala, the lateral septal area the prefrontal cortex and he lateral hypothalamus, dopamine being the responsible neurotransmitter for this pleasure cycle. .

Furthermore it is this same cortico-striatal-thalamic-cortical loop that is responsible for impulsiveness. There is an increase of dopamine and a decrease of serotonin in highly impulsive and aggressive behaviors. The increase in dopamine will decrease inhibition and control and stimulates impulsive behavior.

A person without a proper level of emotional intelligence will be more instinctive, stubborn and fickle when it comes to what he thinks he likes or needs, always dissatisfied in spite of reaching their objective. Training your emotional intelligence would enable you to know what you need, want and desire. Prioritize it in line with one's own capabilities, the possibility of achieving it short or long term and drive you to its accomplishment maintaining and persisting in the behavior necessary to reach it.

One of the signs of a properly developed emotional intelligence is the ability to communicate to others your own emotions. This requires proper use of language whether it is verbal or written and also be accompanied by non-verbal language.

Development of language skill improves progressively with practice, from the first syllables uttered at 6 months of age then moving on to the first words said at 11 or 12 months, until a child arrives at 18 months where there are about a dozen words that are easily pronounced and can be used to form fairly complex phrases. After that with practice, and above all exposure to people, the vocabulary becomes enriched and refined until it reaches an "acceptable" level with which a person communicates with others.

Regarding the neural foundations of language, even though there were records about the location of the mental functions of the brain or more specifically its ridges and groves, it was not until the XIX century when Broca spoke about the location of the language function, in the left inferior frontal gyrus. This area was named after him and is now know also known as Broca's area.

Around the same time Wernicke confirmed the data related to the biological substrate of the language in the cerebral hemispheres, adding a new location for language comprehension in the left superior temporal gyrus, this region is now known as Wernicke's area.

Regarding communication through the language of emotions, these are learned as speech is developed. An example of this is poetry.

Those who have not sufficiently developed their emotional intelligence find it hard to express their feelings whether through words or actions. This ability can be developed in order to improve the vocabulary so as to be able to "find the right words" that are adequate for each situation.

Chapter 3. Emotional intelligence in school

Emotions are present when a baby is born or even before birth but these are very basic and mostly related to physiological needs.

Little by little, and as experiences are made, secondary emotions begin to emerge. Those emotions are related to learning even though the child is hardly aware of it.

Emotional intelligence begins to emerge as a social ability that is "corrected" with practice and related to the values and customs of the place of development. It is through adolescence that these emotions are put to the test as they are subjected to hormonal, physiological and psychological changes.

As the body of the adolescent changes, so do their emotions, since these are closely linked to how a person sees themselves and others. These elements are not always stable and fluctuate with time.

The youth begins to be treated as an "adult" and is expected to assume certain responsibilities and rights in social circumstances. The family ceases to be the point of reference such now shifting to their circle of friends. At the same time there are "feelings" awakened that have been unknown until now related to love and sexuality.

Regarding self image, attitudes and thinking development, these will vary over time so that what was at one time okay is now disgusting. At the same time as the youth tries to understand and face this new world of emotions that is opening before them to which they are especially sensitive due to the increase of hormones in the blood stream.

Feelings of uncertainty, disappointment, confusion, or insecurity among others arise very easily since they have not quite developed the personality that would enable them to adequately defend themselves against external demands.

Also, there may be feelings of loneliness, thinking that "no one understands me" which could lead to the onset of symptoms of depression.

This is a time when emotions are felt at their strongest. Thus it is common to see young ones at rallies and protests, sometimes even resulting in violent acts. On the opposite spectrum, there are those who feel identified by NGOs and other humanitarian institutions and invest time and effort involved in such.

Keep in mind that the scale of personal values is still being developed some of which, with the passing of time, could become superfluous. In the same manner, moral standards are also being established and this is the reason why in adolescence everything has a "justification" as long as it is for a "good cause".

Something that could result in conflictive and even sometimes anti-social behaviors is the idea that "this is not how I choose to live my life"and therefore, "I will not conform" as it seems that adults so often do.

This is a mix of rebellion, identity search, and exploring the limits of society, which begins to diminish with time as the moral development of the youth progresses.

In this stage of development some adolescents overestimate their potential and are "moved" by hedonistic motivations searching only for the things that give them pleasure and satisfaction and running away from everything that carries responsibility or that requires effort.

During this phase the way that emotions are experiences changes as well as learning how to express these emotions in an appropriate manner and to interpret the emotions of others correctly.

In this time period it is easy to "mistake" the "signals" of the opposite sex since this is a language that has to be developed and learned gradually.

This development occurs as a result of past learning processes where the children of parents that have provided an enriching emotional formation exhibit fewer problems adapting to their new situation.

This new situation comes with new responsibilities

concerning life, emotions and thoughts and at the same time this role of "child", where everything is done for you, is gradually left behind.

But if this is the natural development of an adolescent there are times when they have to face situations that include humiliation, vexation and even maltreatment in school by their classmates as is the case in bullying.

The most common disorders affecting youth are anxiety disorders, depression and also phobias.

In spite of the aforementioned the responsibility does not always lie entirely on the shoulders of the adolescent. When parents have suffered some type of psychological disorder they fear their children may experience the same things they went through in terms of the illness, diagnosis and treatment.

Even though not all mental illnesses have a high rate of heredity, there is an increased percentage of possibility that a child will exhibit some form of psychological pathology in the case that one of the parents have suffered from it.

If the cause cannot be explained by a genetic basis then it can be explained by the environment in which the child is raised. The child may have been a "witness"of the episodes of the illness of one of their parents which may serve as a "model"for behavior. Likewise, the way that a person who suffers from a mental illness raises a child may not be the best or "healthiest"for that child which could plant the seed that could be the foundation for future psychopathology when the child grows up.

It has been observed, in the case of parents who suffer from anxiety disorders or major depression, that there is a significant increase in the incidence of their children being affected by the same disorders. To put it plainly, children of anxious parents exhibit higher levels of anxiety, even to the point of being pathological, and together with depression this becomes a major depression disorder. But to what extent can a parent forewarn the presence of the same symptomatology in their child?

This is the subject of research by the Groningen University, the Leiden University Medical Center (Netherlands), and VU University Medical center (Amsterdam) published in 2014 in the scientific journal BMC Psychology.

Participating in the study were 25 parents who had suffered a unipolar mania or anxiety who had children between the ages of 8 and 18. All had to undergo a semi structured interview about various subjects, their way of educating their children and the psychological health of their children.

Results indicate that even though the parents feel they are offering the same quality of care and attention to their children as any other parent, they still worry about the presence or lack of symptoms that they themselves have suffered as part of their mental illness.

Almost all the parents agree that their children should have specialized attention as a preventive measure and to prevent the illness from worsening as soon as they exhibit the first symptoms that could indicate that there is a possibility they may be suffering from the same mental illness as them.

A particularly controversial issue was that of if they would share with their children that they themselves had suffered from mental illness. This groundbreaking study highlights the fears of parents who have suffered from mental illness but due to the low number of participants, and the interview being only semi structured does not allow for obtaining extrapolatable conclusions.

However, we must recognize there is a lack of educational courses targeted to this group that could help them in the upbringing of their children so they can properly identify the first symptoms of their own illnesses and with that alleviate the fear they have about the psychological health of their children.

Keep in mind that there are many aspects that could be included in emotional intelligence. In a society preoccupied with individual results sometimes we "turn our backs" to the development of one of these aspects, compassion.

Compassion is viewed in many cultures as a human "weakness". But if we stop to think, this is precisely what separates us from most animals.

When we see an elderly, sick or disabled person, this compassion is "activated" within us and we are prompted to want to help and provide protection. This is something that has been observed even in our ancestors. Archaeologists have found people buried who have had their broken bones mended, an indication that the group attended to and took care of the afflicted individual for sufficient time for them to heal.

Compassion is what moves us to act with solidarity when there is social upheaval or catastrophe and strangers receive help from total strangers.

Compassion is a protection against negative emotions such as anxiety, anger and fear, promoting friendship and social relations.

It is also an element that is closely related to empathy, which is the ability to understand the emotions of others and put ourselves in their place and that at the same time is present in our everyday life and that we can use in lesser or greater measure depending on our emotional development. Who is more compassionate, men or women?

This question is being investigated by the Department of Communication at the University of California the results have been published in the Journal of Happiness and Well-Being.

This study was participated in by 613 university students between the ages of 18 and 42, 10 of which were women.

All were given a series of standardized questionnaires; to evaluate the level of compassion they used the Compassion Scale, for evaluating the level of anxiety at the moment of communication they used the Personal Report of Communication Apprehension (PRCA-24), to evaluate the level of neuroticism they used the Hypersensitive Narcissism Scale (HSNS), and lastly, to measure the personality trait of verbal aggressiveness they used the Verbal Aggressiveness Scale (VAS) level of aggressive.

The results show a significant difference in compassion based on gender, women having a higher level of it.

There also found significant differences in levels of communication anxiety and verbal aggressiveness with men showing higher levels of both.

Lastly, there were no differences found in narcissism in relation to gender.

Looking at factors of interaction it was discovered that the more compassionate people exhibited lower anxiety levels when communicating and lower levels of verbal aggressiveness and narcissism.

Some of the limitations of the study are that it was only questionnaire based, and did not utilize other types of observation

The study also did not take into account the level of emotional intelligence of the subjects, a key factor in the development of interpersonal relationships; neither was the level of alexithymia evaluated which would indicate the capacity of a person to perceive the emotions of others and respond adequately.

Likewise, as the author of the investigation herself points out, the verification of these significant differences is not accompanied by theories that explain said differences or show the implications associated with them.

The author also indicates that in future investigations they have yet to analyze the different types of compassion, according to the level of emotional bond or affection between the parties and also self compassion.

In spite of the aforementioned limitations, everyday there are new studies that prove there are differences between men and women, without saying one is better or worse than the other or looking to demean either one.

That having been said the cultivating of compassion through the development of emotional intelligence will cause individuals to have fewer verbally aggressive behaviors and communication anxiety.

Far from making us "weaker" this will enable us to establish more solid and lasting bonds of affection, friendship or intimacy at the same time as have improved, closer and more direct communication without personal stress or tension and without the need to use aggressiveness in verbal communication.

When we talk about intelligence we tend to speak of it as something static in time, someone who was born with a certain intellectual quotient which will stay with them for the rest of their lives. In spite of this, educational institutions make great efforts to increase the "level" of their students hoping to improve their intelligence through education. But, is the same level of intelligence maintained throughout a person's life?

There was an investigation of this question carried out by the Western Illinois University and Loyola Marymount University. The results have been published in the Journal of Intelligence.

The data was taken from a Murray Research Archive longitudinal multifactorial study that analyzes participants through 30 years, taking data from 177 participants when they were 3 or 4, 11, 18, and 32 years old. All of them were given multiple standardized questionnaires over time. For this study however, only the information related to the Q-Sort, the High Intellectual Capacity item of the California Child Q-Set, and the development of academic skills through the Wechsler Preschool and primary Scale of Intelligence was used. They also took into account other variable such as the gender of the participants, and the socio-economic level and education of their parents.

The results show a significant relation between initial intelligence levels and those developed through time evaluated in the academic performance.

Even though the study is very clear as to the ability to predict intelligence it does not evaluate the role that education plays in intelligence and how having a high or low level of education corresponds with the levels of intelligence whether high or low, which would validate the efforts of the educational institutions, or could call those efforts into question if there is no relation found between education levels and intelligence.

Also, the study is only focused on academic intelligence, in other words, the ability to adequately respond to the demands and expectations of the educational institutions in each one of the educational levels, forgetting the dimensional approach that affirms that a person can have a normal academic performance attributed to a normal intelligence and yet excel and even be a genius in other fields such as artistic, social, etcetera, that because of their "uselessness" to the educational institutions are not evaluated or encouraged by providing what the student would need. What happens with emotional intelligence?

When we think about emotions they do not seem to be something static as they change over time and even depending on who you are dealing with you could feel one way or another and interpret what they are saying positively or negatively depending on who you are talking to.

You may laugh at a friend's jokes, but that same joke, but coming from a stranger the same joke may not have the same humorous effect. In addition, the passage of time can change our emotional experience. As we have more experiences we learn how to face different emotional situations whether they are positive or negative. This means that as we learn how to act in certain circumstances we are less affected by the emotions generated by such, as has been believed for a long time now.

Meanwhile, there has been researched developed that analyzes the influence of emotions on health. For example, a "strong" or shocking emotion could trigger temporary disturbances in a person and with time that person will recover from the "impact". However, this research is primarily focused on positive emotions in hopes to reinforce the optimal conditions to promote positive emotions in specific ages, especially those who are elderly or very advanced in age.

The Carnegie Mellon University has conducted research on how upsetting situations affect the elderly. The results have been published in the scientific journal Health Psychology. This study involved 6,817 persons over 50 years old who had participated in the previous longitudinal Health and Retirement Study carried out between 2006 and 2010.

All were given diverse standard questionnaires about their health; number and severity of times they were upset and the source whether it was from their mate, children, or other family members or friends; and their emotional state as a result. In addition, their blood pressure was taken. The results were compared with expected standards according to their age and previously established sociodemographic state.

The subjects who had high blood pressure and those who were on medication for stress were excluded from the study.

Results indicate that age does not protect and individual from being upset rather, it makes one more sensitive to negative emotions. That is what was concluded by the researchers when after 4 years of study 29% of the participants developed high blood pressure related 38% to experiencing negative emotions. This relation becomes higher in women between 50 and 65 years of age and becomes especially impactful when these upsetting situations come from family or friends.

Even though the results appear clear there are still 62% of the cases of high blood pressure not explained by negative emotions arising from being upset. Likewise the differences between men and women have been pointed out but not been explained satisfactorily as to what the source could be, whether it is a biological reason, the actual experience, or other factors that "protect" the stress level of men facing these upsetting experiences and that by contrast affect women in such a negative fashion that it affects their health. The results, however limited, are clear in that it is important to adequately take care of and look after the elderly since they are just as emotional, if not more so, than the rest and their health could be adversely affected by such experiences. In view of that it is important to protect them from upsetting experiences that could trigger negative emotions in them.

Up to now emotional intelligence has been presented as the ability to handle our emotions properly, the positive emotions as well as negative, which will play a prominent role in the way we feel, think, and act.

In contrast, those who have low levels emotional intelligence will stand out by their high levels of alexithymia since some authors indicate that it is rather a continuum.

It has been observed that persons with high levels of alexithymia can develop antisocial behaviors sometimes through exposure to risk-taking behavior for themselves or for others where the consequences of that behavior on their health or even personal integrity are evident.

When we think about risk-taking behavior we generally tend to imagine very extreme behaviors such as driving at very fast speeds or bungee jumping. But just as risky for a person's health are behaviors that do not draw as much attention such as smoking or abuse of alcohol or other drugs. What role does emotional intelligence play in risk-taking behavior?

This is precisely what is being investigated at the Universidad de Oviedo (Spain). The results have been published in the Journal of Nursing Education. The subjects of the study were 275 students from the nursing department.

All were assessed their emotional intelligence levels by means of the standardized Schutte Emotional Intelligence Scale.

Risk-taking conduct was evaluated in terms of use of tobacco, alcohol, and illegal drugs as well as having a poor diet, whether they were overweight or not, were sedentary or not, degree of exposure to the sun, and practice of unprotected sex. Furthermore, sociodemographic and life satisfaction data was collected.

The results indicate that the students who had high levels of emotional intelligence exhibited decreased risk-taking behavior such as moderate alcohol consumption, not practicing unhealthy eating habits and engaging in protected sex.

Conversely, those with lower emotional intelligence levels which would correspond with higher levels of alexithymia displayed much higher risk-taking behavior such as excessive alcohol consumption, following an unhealthy diet and practicing unprotected sex.

There were not significant differences in behaviors towards tobacco or illegal drug use, their weight, if sedentary or not, or level of sun exposure in relationship to their level of emotional intelligence.

The authors point out the benefits that higher emotional intelligence has when it comes time to adequately deal with peer pressure, especially having to do with alcohol consumption.

It bears pointing out that the study only gathers information regarding risk-taking behavior by means of self-reporting which leaves open the possibility of influencing factors such as the need for social likability when giving the answers, saying what is sociably acceptable, without corroborating whether or not this is the actual behavior in real life.

Likewise, by using a specific population, in this case university students, it does not allow for extrapolations as to how other young people would behave.

In spite of the aforementioned limitations, the results seem clear as to the advantage of educating young people to have a well developed emotional intelligence since this will help them to avoid future risk-taking behaviors.

Chapter 4. Benefits of Emotional Intelligence

The concept of emotional intelligence has to do with a capacity that can be developed and nurtured. The development of emotional intelligence allows us to have better control of our emotions and improves our social relations.

It is not a matter of controlling our emotions in the sense of "repressing" them, but rather knowing which situations generate what feelings and know how to respond appropriately.

There is certainly a stage in which emotions flare up in some cases in an uncontrolled fashion presenting themselves in a changing and unstable manner, this is adolescence.

This stage is especially sensitive for the youth who is trying to find their identity, also developing their self esteem in relationship to their own values and those of others while dealing with the hormonal and physical changes that occur during puberty. Is it known whether emotional intelligence affects life satisfaction?

The answer to this question is being researched by the Department of Guidance and Counseling, Faculty of Education, Duzce University, the Department of Guidance and Counseling, Faculty of Education, Necmettin Erbakan

University and the Department of Guidance and Counseling, Faculty of Education, Yildiz Technical University. The results were published in the scientific journal Psychology.

The study group includes 319 university students, ages ranging between 17 to 21 years, 68.3 of which were female.

All received the standard questionnaire for the evaluation of level of emotional intelligence through the Trait Emotional Intelligence Questionnaire SF, the Life Satisfaction Scale and the Core-Self Evaluation Scale, the latter measures core-self evaluation levels, self-sufficiency, internal locus of control, and emotional stability (neuroticism).

Results show that there is a significant and positive relation between emotional intelligence, life satisfaction and core-self evaluation.

It bears pointing out that all the tests are based on what each participant knows or thinks about themselves and reported in self-reports.

To conclude the study it is important to include other factors such as the academic performance, and the opinion of others about the participants as complementary measures.

Furthermore, and in spite of the large number of participants the study is focused on a specific population,

Turkish university students, who have characteristics typical of their culture which makes it difficult to extrapolate the results to other populations. This makes it necessary to carry out another investigation in order to have conclusive results.

In spite of the limitations of the study the researchers have successfully explored the levels of core-self evaluation and personal satisfaction as specific elements necessary for the development of emotional intelligence.

In other words, being happy with who you are and what you do during adolescence depends on the level of emotional intelligence you possess.

Likewise, having a positive self-concept, adequate self-sufficiency about our own capabilities, an adjusted internal locus of control and proper emotional stability will depend on the level of emotional intelligence of young university students.

All this reinforces the idea of the need of educational intervention in primary school and high school so that learning how to manage emotions can have a positive effect throughout the life of the student.

When we think about school we tend to think about a place where students learn and are formed without major problems, but this period produces the most important changes not only physical but also psychological in adolescence and thus school could become a "problem".

The search for identity or of belonging to a group sometimes could be the most important thing in life for young people in the developing stage.

Educational centers are characterized by being able to evaluate levels of development.

The idea is to "force" students to be up to date with their studies, and exams are designed to see how far they have come and to know if they are behind or not in relationship with the rest of the class.

But this evaluation could become a source of stress in what has been labeled Test Anxiety. Therefore, does NLP have application is school?

This question is being researched by the Department of Biomechanics and Motor Behavior, College of Sports Science and Physical Activity (Saudi Arabia). The results have been published in the International Journal of Behavioral Research & Psychology.

The study included 30 students, all male, with an average age of 19 years old, half of which received stress control through NLP, the rest did not. This was the control group.

The intervention group trained with the NLP technique for 3 months, two sessions per week each lasting between 40 to 60 minutes.

The level of test anxiety was evaluated in both groups before and after training using a Likert type scale with 96 items.

Blood pressure and BPM was also measured to complement the evaluation of anxiety levels.

Results show significant differences in stress reduction in the students that received the NLP training. The control group showed no change in both the subjective and objective evaluation.

One of the limitations of the investigation is that they only selected male participants for the study. This makes it difficult to ascertain if the effectiveness of NLP to reduce levels of anxiety in students is different based on gender.

Also, choosing to use NLP techniques is not sufficiently substantiated since there are many other techniques that could have been used to achieve the same objective.

In spite of the aforementioned limitations it seems clear that anxiety can be reduced and controlled in students if the right tools are available to them.

Keep in mind that besides the home, school is the second place where students spend the most time. Therefore it seems logical to think that it should be a place where they should feel at ease and not stressed.

This is why research such as the one we just

highlighted is useful to help us remember how, with barely 3 months training, a student can be helped while they are in the educational system offering them a positive and pleasant experience.

All this thanks to the application of stress control techniques that can help to improve emotional intelligence.

Chapter 5. Resiliency in School

Resiliency is an ability that can be learned and developed and that plays a vital role in self protection. We are all exposed to stresses daily but a well developed resiliency enables a person to overcome difficulties as they arise thus the importance of teaching it in school.

There was a boom in the 80s about emotional psychology and in particular its applied branch of emotional intelligence. This spawned the development of a vocabulary so specific that sometimes we are not familiar with all of it. An example of this is the term Resilience which could be understood as a combination of personal skills and abilities that a person has to face the most difficult situations and come out victorious.

Even though some have identified it as a personal quality that we may be born with such as charisma, it is mainly considered that it is something that can be trained and improved in order to have the tools necessary to handle everyday life. Thus resiliency is something that, as we have seen, is necessary to have for any job or profession. Then, at which age is it appropriate to learn to increase resilience?

This is exactly what is being researched at the University of Hong Kong whose results have been published in the Universal Journal of Health.

There were 257 students who participated in the study, 86% were between the ages of 16 and 20 and the rest were over 20.

All were given a series of questionnaires to ascertain their levels of stress, if there were physical symptoms associated with stress, if there was depression, level of self-confidence, self-esteem and optimism.

The results indicate that more than half of the participants consider themselves as having a good level of resiliency together with adequate levels of self-esteem and personal self-control.

Regarding gender differences where half the participants were female, there were higher levels of anxiety and stress together with lower social perception among them.

Likewise, students coming from a single parent household were evaluated. This only proved to be 10% of the cases. They were observed as having lower levels of resiliency and self esteem as compared to their peers.

This data is somewhat worrisome due to the fact that half the students showed low resiliency which is something that can be trained and that proves very useful not only for increasing self esteem but also in academic performance. In addition, just as the authors of the study indicate, low resiliency could bring on sleep disorders associated with anxiety and other psychosomatic issues.

This study reminds us that these are adolescents in the developing stages and just as much as the educational institutions concern themselves with having children practice sports for their physical development it would also be appropriate to establish programs to teach emotional resiliency with which they can improve their emotional intelligence and thus make it easier for them to be able to deal with anxiety and stress, something that seems to affect girls a lot more than boys and that even though it has been found in previous studies it does not seem to be sufficiently explained.

In the critical stages of development where there are continuous changes something like divorce or separation of the parents could be an important factor in stress.

This stress may be accompanied by many symptoms such as sadness, fear, anxiety, feelings of abandonment, anger and a desire for reconciliation of the parents. All of this is also reflected in lower academic performance, losing interest for academic activities, which produce feelings of unhappiness.

This only complicates the process of divorce even more. Each parent lives separately and the adolescent is forced to visit them separately sometimes weekly, depending on what they have agreed on or what the court imposes as visitation when the parents cannot come to a mutual agreement.

This adult situation, though seemingly peaceful, still has physical and psychological consequences on the adolescent but when it is not peaceful it will certainly have even greater consequences at times turning the adolescent into a go-between and at the same the victim of the conflicting and negative feelings of the parents without being at fault of the reason or the development of the divorce to begin with.

But the aforementioned feelings and the subsequent unhappiness are not always present in all cases, sometimes the adolescent's maturity is involved, the degree of family conflict, and even the prolonged absence of one of the parents. There are also other factors at play such as the personality of the adolescent or the degree of resiliency that would help protect them from the stress caused by this type of situation. How does divorce affect adolescents?

This subject is being studied at the University of Bolu Atatürk and the University of Abant Izzet Baysal (Turkey). The results have been published in the scientific journal Psychology.

This study had 144 adolescent participants, 75 of which were girls.

All were given three standard scales. One was for

evaluating the feelings of loneliness and abandonment, Loneliness Scale. Another was for feelings of happiness, Life Satisfaction Scale. And another evaluated the levels of resiliency, Adolescents Resiliency Scale.

The results indicate a significantly negative relation between feelings of happiness and loneliness; a significantly negative relation between resiliency and loneliness; and a significantly positive relation between feelings of happiness and resiliency.

It was observed that the onset of feelings of loneliness happens only due to low feelings of happiness and resiliency. Feelings of loneliness may be considered a predicting factor of future problems associated with divorce which need to be addressed, evaluated and treated before they turn into major problems for adolescents.

In spite of the clarity of the data, the research lacks a control group with which to establish if the levels of feelings of loneliness, happiness or resiliency are greater or lesser than the population of youths whose parents have not divorced.

There is something worth highlighting in the study and that is the importance of cultivating important factors such as feelings of happiness or resiliency in order to avoid the onset of sadness and feelings of abandonment in adolescents whose parents have divorced.

As we have seen, resiliency as part of emotional intelligence is fundamental to overcome situations in daily life but also those that could potentially scar an adolescent such as the divorce of his parents.

Chapter 6. Intervening in Emotional Intelligence

Keeping in mind we are talking about emotion which could be defined as changes in mood, sometimes temporary, they could be pleasant or unpleasant (valence) and that could cause changes in cognition and in the body depending on its intensity (arousal).

There are various classifications of emotions. Thus they can be divided between innate or primary emotions (fear, happiness, sadness, surprise, disgust, or anger) and learned or secondary emotions (guilt, pride, shame, jealousy, or envy). The function of emotion could be divided in, adaptive (responding to environment); social (promoting social relationships); and motivational (facilitating the accomplishment of objectives).

Emotions have their own processing pathways through the amygdala which analyzes information more quickly in order to give adaptive responses if necessary before the neocortex becomes "aware" of the situation.

It is also worth noting that emotions perform a number of functions such as:

- Adaptive function, where emotion helps interpret the nature of the stimuli as pleasant or unpleasant (valence), preparing the body to respond if it has to do with something unpleasant that could pose a threat to the individual. On the other hand, a positive valence stimulus will generate an opposite effect motivating the action to go near such stimulus. When faced with uncertainty about a certain stimulus the human brain reacts as it would when faced with danger since it is unable to discern whether it poses a threat or not.

- Social function, Due to the fact that humans are "social animals" emotions will pay a definitive role in how we behave around others. In order to do this the person has to correctly know, understand, analyze and interpret his own emotions as well as learn to express them to others as part of communication that will emphasize and qualify the verbal message. Likewise the emotion of the other party needs to be properly interpreted within the context of the message in order to contribute to communication in which there are no misunderstandings or wrong interpretations.

- Motivational function is where emotion incites and initiates action at the same time as it points it towards its goal influencing at the same time the intensity of response. Therefore, an emotion with low arousal will elicit little response whereas an emotion with high arousal will elicit a response with great intensity as evidenced by a start caused by an unexpected loud noise. Regarding the direction promoted by the emotion, this one can be either of approach or withdrawal from the stimulus. For example, when faced with a potentially dangerous stimulus, our ancestors would could run away, attack, or keep still with the hopes that the danger would go away unseen.

Emotional intelligence would thus assume such functions and in the persons in whom it is developed would carry them out, while those who have not developed it would experience a diminishing in one or more of these functions.

People with high levels of emotional intelligence are more adept at the execution of emotional functions being able to more quickly and with better precision interpret the valence of stimuli (adaptive function). Furthermore, they would be able to know and interpret their own emotions and those of others (social function). They would also feel a great urge to attain that which is pleasant to them (motivational function) giving them the desire and the determination to persevere until they achieve it when it has to do with a high arousal stimulus.

On the other hand, a person with low emotional development will have great difficulty distinguishing between that which is pleasant or unpleasant, including something that could put him in danger (adaptive function). Likewise, he will not know "for sure" what or how he is feeling, nor be able to adequately interpret the emotions of others which would lead him to social incompetence, preferring to be isolated and alone due to his inability to adequately express his emotions (social dysfunction). Also he will not be able to correctly estimate the effort required to realize a stimulus in relationship to its arousal which would result in him "tiring out" too quickly and as a result not reaching his goals, or using too many resources on a goal that is not "worth it" causing a squandering and exhaustion of resources (motivational dysfunction).

An extreme example of these dysfunctions would be persons suffering from alexithymia who Goleman labeled as "emotional illiterates", a trait that seems to affect one in ten men and that attests to the lack of development of emotional intelligence where a person handles themselves "however he can" in an emotional world that he is never able to comprehend or handle adequately not ever knowing what he feels, what others feel or how to express himself at an emotional level.

There are three general objectives for emotional education in the classroom. The first is geared towards knowing your own emotions. The second, to learn to express said emotions in an adequate manner. The third is to interpret the emotions of others.

a) Regarding the first objective, the following exercises could be introduced in the classrooms:

- Explain each one of the emotions
- Illustrate each one of the emotions

- Differentiate emotions in relationship to the activity they generate

- Exercise high activating emotions by means of watching videos

- Exercise low activating emotions by means of watching videos

- Have a group talking session about the feelings experienced after watching the videos

b) Regarding expression of emotions in the classroom:

- Explain the different types of expression of emotions

- Talk about the consequences of anger and aggression on the body

- Explain and identify symptoms of depression in

- Exercise the expression of feelings in a controlled manner

- Exercise the control of emotions such as anger or violence in the classroom

c) Regarding the correct interpretation of the feelings of others, the exercises could be as follows:

- Explain the emotions of another person as well as the body language and gestures that accompany them

- Observe and interpret the emotions of high activity in another person by viewing

- Observe and interpret the emotions of low activity in another person by viewing

- Partner up students and perform an exercise where one chooses an emotion to express and the other tries to guess what it is

- Carry out an exercise with a minimum of three students where each interprets a different emotion to the same event

- Have a group talking session about the emotions observed and expressed by the pairs or mini groups

To illustrate the group talking sessions in practice I will now transcribe the interview I gave to the Government of Canarias (Spain) about the initiative of inclusion of Emotional and Creativity Education in the primary education curriculum.

- What relation is there between emotional education and creativity?

Very much. Creativity has a high emotional component in the sense that we identify with that which we create and the need to feel emotion while creating. And vice versa, our way of relating with others and with ourselves is a way to exhibit our originality to the world.

- Why implement this in primary education curriculum?

All the scientific studies that have been done about emotional education advise to begin as soon as possible. In canaries emotions have a long tradition of work in the stage of Child Education (the curriculum of this stage covers explicitly the need to give attention to the world of affects, feelings and emotions in the youngest children). In primary education it has been more present in terms of programs and activities apart from the teaching staff but we have seen the need to implement them in the curriculum so attend to the needs of the students and the teachers.

- What benefits do you hope to achieve with the implementing of this assignment?

Happier students that know how to identify and regulate their emotions and develop their entire creative potential.

- Is this initiative based on previous ones?

Even though there have been many experiences based on educational programs this is the first time (on a national and international level) that there has been an official curriculum included as its own entity.

- Who would provide this initiative and what relationship does it have with psychology?

We would suggest the tutor but it could also be a person who fits the right profile.

- How would you evaluate the effectiveness of the initiative? Are you looking at an evaluation midway or long term?

Throughout the whole course we are carrying out a qualitative assessment of the process to observe the degree of implementation in the area.

- Have you considered incorporating this subject to more confrontational ages such as the stage of adolescence?

It would be beneficial to include it in later stages. We are researching that possibility.

Chapter 7. Emotional Intelligence and Bullying

The emotional distresses that can occur in the classroom are various; there are envies, misunderstandings or fights that can disturb the normal development in a classroom. But the most critical event that a student can suffer due to the significant effects it can have in their present and future life is bullying.

Bullying is one of the biggest concerns of teachers and psychologists that are endeavoring to avoid its effects on the children that are victims of it. Is it possible to avoid the harmful effects of bullying with intervention on the Theory of Mind of students?

Imagine waking up in the morning and your mother tells you that you need to go to a school where you know you will come across children who will harass, bully, insult and hit you. Would you go to class?

This is a reality that more and more children in school have to face. What is the solution? At the moment, it is not known if there is one. If there was, all the students who suffer bullying would be "exported" to the rest of the centers in the education system thus alleviating a reality that has been confirmed leaves deep emotional "scars" in the children who will suffer from its consequences even into adulthood.

It goes beyond the bumps and bruises, and other

"minor" injuries that a student may suffer. The most serious ones are precisely the ones that cannot be seen, the ones at the psychological level. These are the ones that will undermine the child's self esteem in a phase that is critical for personality development which will determine in large measure how this child will relate to others in the future. It could become such a stressful situation that it could even be the source of psychosomatic illnesses such as suicide attempts in the worst cases.

To give answer to this question there have been many attempts at giving direct intervention and therapy for those that are bullied, or for the ones doing the bullying, or the teachers so they can identify bullying situations in the classroom and even be able to "stop" it. The authority of the teachers has been increased as well as the consequences of inappropriate behavior in class, and even offering talks geared towards raising awareness in parents so they can identify when a child is exhibiting symptoms that "something is not right" in school. All these interventions have had different results but as was pointed out in the beginning there is an adequate formula to "nip in the bud" this ever growing problem.

A joint study by the University of Milano-Bicocca (Italy) and the University of Manitoba (Canada) who published their results in the Journal of Experimental Child

Psychology which address this matter from a different perspective.

The authors understand that by the time bullying occurs in school it is already too late and that it is better to notice previous stages of development with which to work with so these types of situations do not occur in the first place. In other words, the "cure" consists in prevention.

The research involved 110 participants between the ages of 6 and 7 years, half of which were girls.

The participants were assigned at random one of the experimental groups. Over the course of two months, both groups were made to read a series of paragraphs about emotional situations. The first group was asked to comment on the paragraphs openly about the nature, causes and regulations of the emotions, while the second group was asked to draw what they thought.

The results show that the first group increased their understanding of emotions, the Theory of Mind (putting yourself in someone else's shoes), as well as empathy, when evaluated after the training phase. These results lasted even six months after the training was over.

Even though the chance of future occurrences of bullying were not evaluated, the authors hope that a better understanding of their own emotions, and empathy would be "enough" to prevent bullying in the future. This shows that lack of empathy and impulse control would be at the core of disruptive behavior on the part of the young bully.

An attempt to diminish the "devastating" effects of bullying in school before it arises from the perspective of education in infancy, a model that proves to be "exportable" to other places, would be beneficial for children since it "guarantees" a better social behavior without resorting to bullying.

In this regard I will now transcribe and interview I had with Dr. Noelia Carbonell Bernal who wrote her thesis on this subject:

- What is the incidence of bullying in schools?

In Spain it is estimated that it hovers between 15 – 20 percent.

- Can bullying in school be prevented?

It can and it should, but it is necessary to include and raise awareness in all the players involved, especially the students and teachers.

- Why is emotional intelligence important in the case of bullying in schools?

Emotional intelligence s very important, it includes important aspects such as empathy, which is the ability to put ourselves in someone else's shoes, and assertiveness, which is the ability that humans have to enforce our rights without harming others. Learning these abilities together with important aspects such as self control, we achieve that the subjects involved in these bullying dynamic, observers, aggressors and victims, can resolve their problems in an emotionally intelligent manner and avoid aggressiveness, physical as well as verbal.

Even so, and more generally speaking, we can claim that the students who have participated in our program appreciate in a very positive way the activities that have been conducted during the course of the program.

- What characteristics would the implementation of an Emotional Intelligence Program have in the case of bullying in schools?

The CIE (Convivencia e Inteligencia Emocional) Program [Coexistence and Emotional Intelligence] is divided in 5 sessions in which each one of the components of emotional intelligence is explained to the students before moving on to working with them on a practical level. This is conducted through a series of 2 or 3 tasks to execute throughout each session by means of the exercises proposed.

The purpose of the 5 modules that the CIE Program is divided in help give the students strategies to improve their previous levels of emotional intelligence with the goal of preventing and/or intervening in situations of bullying that may have already been detected whether inside or outside of the school.

The ultimate objective of the program is the prevention of school violence detected in the institutions and that these situations of aggression that have been discovered would decrease beginning with the ESO (Obligatory Secondary School Education) just as we have presented here, together with learning the correct use of the elements that make up emotional intelligence.

- What is the effectiveness of an Emotional Intelligence Program in the case of bullying in schools?

The program has accomplished a decrease in the percentage of participators in these types of behaviors of aggression and bullying, both for attackers and victims.

- Starting at what age is it recommended to implement programs of emotional intelligence to prevent bullying in schools?

The CIE intervention program has been designed for application in the adolescent population. However many of its activities can be adjusted to fit other age profiles whether above or below that specified age range.

The CIE Program is geared primarily for students of the 1st and 2nd grade of the ESO (Equivalent in the USA to 7th and 8th grade, or Middle School students), since in these grades where children begin their secondary school is where there is a higher incidence of violence among students and it is for this reason that this program helps in the coexistence of these groups.

Conclusion

This book presents the need to pay attention to emotions in the school environment. In order to do this we need to know which the main problems that arise are and how to solve them.

Emotional intelligence has proven to be a useful tool to prevent many of these problems that students may suffer. Therefore, it is important to learn about its benefits. But above all know how to conduct interventions in the classroom to improve emotional intelligence in school.

About Dr. Juan Moisés de la Serna

Doctor of Psychology, Master in Neuroscience and Behavioral Biology, Clinical Hypnosis Specialist. Recognized by the International Biographical Center (Cambridge – UK) as one of the top one hundred health professionals in the world in 2010. He also teaches in various national and international universities

Scientific disseminator participating in congresses, conferences and seminars; collaborator in various papers, digital media and radio programs; author of the blog "Cátedra Abierta de Psicología y Neurociencias" [Open Chair on Psychology and Neurosciences], and seventeen books on diverse subjects.

Currently he conducts research in the field of Big Data applications in healthcare utilizing data from India, United States and Canada, among others, work which he complements with consultancy to technological startups geared towards psychology and personal wellbeing.